DRESDEN

DRESDEN

A Survivor's Story

February 1945

Victor Gregg
with
Rick Stroud

BLOOMSBURY READER
LONDON · OXFORD · NEW YORK · NEW DELHI · SYDNEY

BLOOMSBURY READER
Bloomsbury Publishing Plc
50 Bedford Square, London, WC1B 3DP, UK

BLOOMSBURY, BLOOMSBURY READER and the Bloomsbury Reader
logo are trademarks of Bloomsbury Publishing Plc

First published in Great Britain in 2013 by Bloomsbury Reader
This edition published in 2019

A catalogue record for this book is available from the British Library

Library of Congress Cataloguing-in-Publication data has been applied for

ISBN: PB: 978-1-4482-1748-9; eBook: 978-1-4482-1145-6

2 4 6 8 10 9 7 5 3

Typeset by Deanta Global Publishing Services, Chennai, India
Printed and bound in Great Britain by CPI Group (UK) Ltd,
Croydon CR0 4YY

MIX
Paper from
responsible sources
FSC® C020471
FSC
www.fsc.org

To find out more about our authors and books visit www.bloomsbury.com
and sign up for our newsletters

To the women and
children of Dresden

CONTENTS

NOTE OF REMEMBRANCE

I wasn't new to murder and bloodletting, I had enlisted two years prior to the outbreak of the Second World War. By the time I was twenty-one I had taken part in one major battle and various smaller ones. I had been in fights where the ground in front of me, as far as the eye could see, was littered with the remains of what had been, a few hours earlier, young men, full of the joy of living, laughing and joking with their mates. These young men were the enemy, or at least, had been.

As each year of the war went by the fighting got more ferocious, new weapons were introduced and fresh young men became the targets. Through all this I somehow remained a sane person. I returned to England in late 1943. After fighting in North Africa and then Italy I rebadged as a member of the 10th Parachute Regiment, bound for the shores of Britain.

Home in England and lauded right left and centre as a hero, which I knew I wasn't, I got married to a girl I had met on my embarkation leave way back in 1937. I was full of beans with not a care in the world; I had experienced so much that I thought of myself as indestructible. After all, I was still in one piece, whereas a whole load of the lads I had joined up with were now laying doggo under a stinking desert sun.

And then, as if it was all part of some great plan, in September 1944 I was hurled from a plane with a few thousand other men, the majority of whom were much younger than myself and had never fired a shot in anger. We were to fight the battle of Arnhem. For the next seven days the small fields and hedgerows of the battlefield became strewn with the dead and mangled bodies of British and German young men, all going to their final resting place in the belief that they were offering themselves up as a sacrifice for the good of mankind. It all left me unaffected, my mind was conditioned by military life to accept that killing your fellow man was normal.

In the end we lost the battle and the lucky ones that survived were marched into captivity laughing and joking, not a bit downhearted. The fact that the fields through which we were marched away had become one huge cemetery didn't cause me, or the lads with me, any undue concern. We thought that this was what war was all about – men killing men, each of us determined to be the last man standing.

Along with another small group of the lads captured at Arnhem I landed up at an *Arbeitslager*, a work camp in a small insignificant German village to the south of the beautiful city of Dresden. The work consisted of cleaning the streets, working in the fields pulling crops from the ground and sometimes shovelling coal for the railways.

We had all volunteered for this work to get away from being shut up in one of the huge POW camps. Even so I made two unsuccessful attempts to escape, after which the camp commandant decided it was time to teach me a short, sharp lesson. He sent me and another bloke, my mate Harry, to work in a soap factory about eight kilometers from the camp. We had to walk there and back every day. This was the beginning of February when the snow came from the skies in the shape and size of dinner plates, so he gave us each a pair of wooden clogs which later on would save my life.

Eventually the two of us managed to sabotage the factory by causing a short circuit in the electrical system. The whole place caught fire and the building collapsed in a crescendo of smoke and flames.

After that we were marched in front of the officer in charge of the police of Dresden. This smart official told us that our fate was out of his hands. There were strict penalties for sabotage, we were to be taken to a place where we would wait our turn, along with other poor sods, to be executed. For the first time since I had joined the army I felt the floor moving. This sod was going to have the pair of us shot. Harry didn't seem to care, 'Something will turn up' said he, and something did.

GRIM TRUTH

Next we were taken by car to a building that stood in a paved square right slap bang in the centre of Dresden. Then we were frog-marched up a set of stone steps under a brick archway, and thrown into a long wide room which extended the length and breadth of the building; it was full of prisoners. Above the heads of these luckless men was a large domed roof made of glass. The place was so crowded that at first glance it seemed impossible to find a place to sit. In the centre of this den of iniquity were two huge forty gallon drums almost full to the brim with excrement, the place stank to high heaven. The other prisoners seemed to have given up any hope of survival, they were a listless and forlorn bunch. The pair of us refused to bow our heads and it wasn't long before we were taking the mickey out the situation. Harry went walkabout and discovered two Americans who were in for looting and like us were awaiting execution. The Yanks, they didn't seem to be too happy about the situation, they told us that the Germans took thirty prisoners away every morning and that's the last anyone ever saw of them.

It must have been well past midday when we first entered this hellhole and soon after we arrived a trolley was pushed into the room by a couple of guards. The Yanks told us that this was the main meal of the day. The inmates fed themselves by putting their open hands into the large container to scoop out with whatever concoction had been served up. Harry and I decided that we weren't that hungry and gave the offering a miss. Day turned into night, and with a push here and a shove there the pair of us managed to claim a small portion of the floor to ourselves. All that was left was to have a kip and await developments on the morrow.

This was the evening of the 13th of February 1945, a date of infamy if ever there was one. At about ten-thirty that night the air-raid sirens started their mournful wailing, and because this happened every night no notice was taken. The people of Dresden thought that as long as the Luftwaffe kept away from Oxford in England then, in return, Dresden would not be bombed. The sirens stopped and after a short period of silence the first wave of pathfinders were over the City dropping their target flares.

From inside the building we saw the flares through the glass cupola, filling the night sky with blinding light, like enormous Christmas trees they floated to earth dripping the burning phosphorus onto the streets and buildings.

As if in slow motion the inmates of the prison began to realise that they were trapped in a cage that stood every chance of becoming a mass grave. The guards had scarpered to what they believed to be a safe hideaway. They had locked and chained the doors from the outside and to cap it all the heavy pulsating throb of hundreds of heavy bombers began to fill the air, and getting nearer and louder by the second.

Harry, who had been chatting to the two Yanks, suggested that it might be a good idea to kick some of the other types away from the wall and for the four of us to get down as low as we could as a means of survival if the worst happened. The wailing of the petrified prisoners who had experienced bombing in other German cities got some of the others in such a state that they were banging on the doors and shouting and crying to be let out, naturally to no effect. As I said before, the guards had all hotfooted it.

The flares were still wending their way to earth when the first of the bomber streams flew over the city, dropping thousands of incendiaries along with which came the first of the bombs. A whole string would hit the ground, one after the other in rapid succession like a drum roll and through the glass cupola the night sky changed from a bright whiteness to a dull red glow that danced, getting brighter and brighter before fading and dying. The bombers passed over in a never ending stream.

By now it was bedlam inside the prison. Then, without any warning, about four incendiaries burst through the heavy glass roof, breaking it into fragments and shredding the luckless men under the cupola into pieces. The phosphorous clung to the bodies of the injured men turning them into human torches. Nothing could be done to help them, it was impossible to extinguish the flames, and so the screaming of those who were being burned alive was added to the cries of the other prisoners. Thanks to Harry the four of us were away from the glass roof and close to the wall, alive and uninjured.

Not for long though. The raid had by now been in progress for the best part of thirty minutes and it must have been one of the last wave that dropped the blockbuster that landed outside of the building, blowing in the whole of the wall. All I could remember was being picked up by a giant hand which threw me over to the far corner of the building, nearly fifty feet. The next thing I knew I was being covered in brickwork and rubble, and everything went dark.

3

OVERTURE TO HELL

I don't think I was unconscious for more than a minute. When I came to I thought that I had been blinded. I could feel a heavy weight on my legs and lower body but my arms were free to move. I managed to clear my eyes of the dust and dirt, then I realised that my eyesight was OK, I could see to the end of my arm. The smoke and fumes from the burning shell of the building was now swept away by the rising force of the wind storm that was gradually increasing.

I managed to free myself from the embrace of the fallen beams and lumps of stonework and stumbled over the debris towards where I had last seen Harry. When I found him he was sitting down against the wall, covered in dust, and motionless. Harry had been overcome by the blast that had hit him full frontal. At this point I reckon that I must have given up all hope, Harry dead and gone, the world around me falling to the ground, surrounded by flames, smoke and dust and the ever increasing heat. I covered Harry up with the coat he had been wearing and managed to stumble outside of the building which by now was slowly collapsing. I found myself, along with the few survivors, in the centre of a huge bonfire.

The first thing that hit me when I emerged from the shaking fabric of the building was the heat. Wherever I turned I was confronted with blocks of debris falling from the sky. The old timber-framed houses were one by one becoming victims of the fire. Once the central beams burnt through, the rest of the structure came crashing to the ground. Most of this wreckage landed on top of the cellars which the inhabitants were using as shelters. The blazing rubble trapped them in man-made ovens where they slowly roasted to death.

There were about a dozen of us in our small group of survivors. We were all in various states of shock, some were screaming with the pain of their injuries and burns, about a dozen of us were more or less fit, that is able to walk or stagger. The problem was where we should go: we were cut off on all sides. I realised that there were other small groups moving between the heaps of rubble, and dodging the flames which, without warning, shot out of gaps in the walls. All the time we watched for the last incendiaries falling from the final wave of bombers. The noise of the planes died down, and it became obvious that the raid had finished. People started to appear from the few houses that were still intact. Survivors were clawing their way to the surface of the huge mounds of rubble that an hour before had been their home.

The flames were growing in intensity. Although the authorities had built huge concrete water containers at points throughout the city only a few of these had been filled with water. But the few that had been filled were later to prove tragic. People climbed into them to escape and found it impossible to climb back out of the smooth-faced concrete. They were trapped in water which slowly boiled.

If there were any fire appliances they could never have traversed the huge mountains of bricks, concrete and burning timber that barred all progress, or the enormous craters that pockmarked the whole ghastly scene.

I was now part of a small group that had bonded as a unit, none of us knowing who the man in front or behind was, we just sort of glued ourselves together as if there was safety in numbers. Slowly we stumbled along the remains of a wide avenue. We were surrounded by fires and mountains of red hot wreckage. What saved me were the wooden clogs that our kindly camp commandant had given me to walk through the snow to the soap factory. The wooden soles of the clogs were so thick I could walk over the red hot cinders and burning rubble that was strewn everywhere.

Finally we found ourselves in open fields, ending up by a single railway line hidden from view down a steep embankment. We had reached safety. Through the dust and smoke we could just make out the outlines of what looked like the main railway station from which a huge column of smoke and fire was climbing into the sky. We still had the problem of the wounded men, some of whom were in a very bad way. I was the odd man out and there wasn't a lot I could do. I couldn't understand a word of the jabbering that was going on around me, so I just kept quiet and followed the herd.

Then we saw another group coming towards us from along the railway line. This lot consisted of about two dozen men in uniform. They were pulling and pushing a large cart. It turned out it was full of picks, shovels, buckets, coils of rope and some cans of drinking water. The leader of the group was the only one with a hat, all the others wore the regulation steel helmet. I reckoned that they were firemen and I was right. The leader immediately had us all form up, selected those men whom he judged to be capable and fit and marched us off. He left the injured to fend for themselves. I don't remember being at all surprised at this action, it seemed like the right thing to do to round up anyone on the loose and make them help wherever was necessary. But not everyone wanted to offer themselves up as fuel to the raging furnace that was burning less than five hundred yards away. When the leader learnt that three of our group were refusing to follow he turned about, pulled a pistol from the holster attached to his belt, and shot two of them at point blank range, the third man started running as fast as he could to catch up with us. There were about thirty of us armed only with picks and shovels making our way back along the same track that we had fled along less than an hour before, led by a German Officer whose answer to a problem was to shoot first and ask questions later.

Thinking back through the years to this episode I cannot fault the action the man took. Chaos reigned everywhere and authority above all else was needed, even if it had to be exerted through the muzzle of a gun. I had been a front line soldier for six years and that is how I had been trained to think.

The leader didn't get it all his own way. The heat stopped us. Even so we came across people who had been caught out in the open and were still alive. By fixing bits of wood to our picks and shovels we turned them into stretchers to carry the injured.

At about midnight, or about two hours after the raid had finished our leader decided that enough was enough. There wasn't much more he could do until the heat lessened and the fires died down so very slowly we trudged back over the burning mounds and made our way back to the original starting point by the railway line. When we reached it we discovered that reinforcements and a food wagon had somehow been shunted in from God knows where.

Then the sirens started their terrible wailing again.

4

SLAUGHTER OF THE INNOCENTS

A lot of survivors from the burning ruins were now out in the open, spread along this low embankment with no shelter or cover of any kind. The inferno was growing fiercer and noisier by the minute, but even so, above the noise I could hear the pulsating throb of hundreds of heavy aircraft bearing down on us. There was no need for flares to lead these bombers to their target, the whole city had become a gigantic torch and must have been visible to the pilots from a hundred miles away. The people around me started to gather in small bunches as if to shield each other from the onslaught. Dresden had no defences, no anti-aircraft guns, no searchlights, nothing. The planes were thousands of feet up but even so it was possible to make out their outlines reflected in the glow of the flames.

As the bombs struck the ground we realised that this second raid had nothing in common with the first raid. The new bombs were so big that it was possible to see them falling through the air. Even the incendiaries were of a different type. Instead of the smallish metre-long sticks that had dropped the first raid, we were now subjected to huge four ton objects that hit the ground and exploded so that a ball of fire blossomed from the point of impact incinerating anything, man-made or human, within a radius of nearly two hundred feet. Raining down with this terror came the blockbusters, thin-walled, ten-ton missiles that demolished whole blocks of buildings in one explosion.

Only five hundred yards of open land separated us from the heart of the first raid on the old part of the city and yet not one bomb landed on us. We laid our bodies down in submission to the slaughter we all sensed was coming. We could feel the terrible heat, our bodies shook as the ground vibrated with the impact as these enormous bombs hit the ground sending great clouds of debris up into the heavens above. As if this was not enough, another terror was making its presence felt.

It wasn't really what you could call a wind or even a gale; the air that was being drawn in from the outside to feed the inferno was like a solid object, so great was its force. The women were clutching onto the men, sensing the danger of being sucked across the open ground into the centre of the enormous bonfire that had once been the centre of Dresden. Further along the line the station was engulfed. I am not certain that this was the main Railway Station of

Dresden but it was a station of sorts. I never got near it, so I cannot say.

It had a centre arch, we could all see, which suddenly collapsed and still not one bomb had landed on the lines leading into the city. As if it was a great car park in the sky, the heavens were full of aeroplanes. As they approached we could hear and see the bombs falling, dropping their loads of death and destruction. On the ground me and my companions were all helpless.

The second raid had been in progress for about a quarter of an hour when halfway between us and the station the ground erupted in huge clouds of smoke and flame. After the concussion came the enormous pull of the wind as air rushed in to replace the vacuum that had been caused by the blasts. It was a very testing time for those of us who could still maintain our composure. It was the officer who again stepped into the breach. He ordered us to move further down the line. In spite of the danger of staying where we were about half of the group, which now numbered about two hundred people, refused to move. We left them, there was nothing to be done for these people who were in a pitiless state, petrified with terror and unable to move their limbs.

Not so our gallant leader, who I believe wanted to take us back into the furnace once the second wave of bombers had concluded their business.

5

AFTERMATH

After half an hour the second wave, much stronger than the first, started to thin out although there were still some stragglers. It was what was happening on the ground that made the difference. Everything was in full flame, everything that could burn was alight including a lot of stuff I thought could never burn. The metalled roadways were like burning rivers of bubbling and hissing tar. Huge fragments of material were flying through the air, sucked into the vortex formed by the hurricane winds.

There were now less than a hundred of us in the group. The position we were in gave us a safe breathing space of roughly two hundred yards from the fires, in some places less. We could see people being torn from whatever they were hanging on to, picked up by an invisible giant hand and drawn up in to the ever-deepening red glow reflected from the clouds of smoke that were swirling around. If we tried to help the heat drove us back, there was nothing we could do.

Try as we might there was no way that we onlookers could bring any assistance to the tragedy that was being played out on the stage.

A small group that had made it almost to the edge of the field tried to reach us, attempting to cross what had once been a roadway, only to get themselves stuck in a bubbling mass of molten tar. One by one these unfortunates sank to the ground through sheer exhaustion and then died in a pyre of smoke and flame.

We watched, as if looking at a giant circus act. People of all shapes, sizes and ages got slowly sucked into the vortex by the force of the winds and then, with a final whisk, they were lifted up into the sky and into the pillars of smoke and fire that carried on up until they disappeared in the clouds above, with their hair and clothing alight. And as if the devil himself decided that the torment the people were suffering was insufficient, above the noise of the wind and the roar of the inferno around us came the interminable, agonised screams of the victims as they were roasted alive. It was these fiendish visions that brutalised my mind in later years.

Then, from out of the smoke and dust a new group joined us with the news that our position was completely cut off. The railway line that we had taken refuge along was now a tangled mass of twisted steel. As each of the buildings to our front collapsed, a new, huge blast of heat enveloped our positions. What saved us was that we were on open ground with oxygen to breathe. But we all knew that although the raids were over, the fires weren't dying down, they were getting worse.

Our leader had given up any idea he may have had about venturing into the furnace that was the once beautiful city of Dresden. The city to our front was now a mass of flame rising up into the night before finally disappearing into the cloud of smoke that filled the heavens above us.

All of us present thought that our last minutes of life were not far away. The heat was intense, but the real horror was the effort it took to breathe, the air was so hot that it was painful to inhale. The leader realised that if we were going to die it was better that we died trying to get away and so with a flourish of his hand he signaled the group to follow him. We did so in silence because the heat made it impossible for us to open our mouths. He led us out to an island of safety and there he called a halt.

I am finding it impossible to describe the scene as it actually was, it had to be witnessed to be believed and those of us that were witnesses would be, for the rest of our lives, affected by the memories of that terrible night.

6

THE GENERAL

As soon as dawn broke through the dark caused by the smoke and flame, we saw that new gangs of men had arrived and were now filling up the huge craters along the railway and relaying the track. By what must have been mid-morning a small line of wagons were shunted up to a position alongside us. You had to hand it to these Krauts, the first thing they think of is invariably their belly. Sure enough in the centre was a kitchen wagon complete with hot soup, black bread and a forty gallon drum of their ersatz coffee, made from crushed acorns.

Yet again our leader sorted out the men he believed would be able to attack his next move into the flames, and I was one of them. He approached me and said 'You Tommy ya?' To which I replied 'Ya, ich bin Englander'. He gave me a grin, 'Gut Englander Tommy, Sie Komm mit eins'. This meant I was to go with him which I didn't mind as it meant food, possible shelter, but most of all he represented order amongst chaos, which I didn't mind, even if he was the hated enemy. If he was brave and stupid enough to fight what I thought was the impossible then I, an Englishman, would match him.

And so that morning of the Fourteenth of February, Nineteen-Forty-Five, our work party of about forty men trudged across the short open field and into the smouldering embers at the edge of the vast bonfire that was still raging less than five or six hundred yards away from us. Other small groups were already digging and shovelling at the piles of fallen masonry, trying to clear a pathway through the rubble so that the rescue gangs could make a start on uncovering the cellars, in the hope that there may be some chance of finding survivors. It must be said that, even though these gangs were made up of different nationalities, everyone set to it with a will.

We had been at it for about half an hour when our leader came over to me. He had noticed that I was struggling and was in pain. He gently lifted my coat and the dried out, brittle shirt from my shoulders to reveal a mass of blisters across my back. He called one of his mates over and must have instructed him to take me to one of the many aid centres that had sprung up just outside the city limits. It was while I was being attended to by a German doctor that the air raid sirens started up again.

This started a minor panic as the little aid centre was right out in the open, with no cover whatever. But the doctor carried on smoothing cream over the blisters on my sore back. Then the third raid started. Now it was the Americans who were flying over us and we reckoned they'd been told about the lack of air defences which, after the bombers had completed their satanic mission, enabled the escorting fighters to come down almost to street level. This time it was the railway yards that were the target. Only a few bombs landed in the burning city centre. It meant that the population who had survived and escaped the night before were now getting the same treatment from the Americans. Luckily the American bombs were much less destructive than the ones the British had used. But, even so, five hundred and one thousand pound bombs kill in the same way that their big brothers, the five and ten thousand pounders, do. In this last raid the tally of the dead continued to rise.

When the raid ended everyone lifted themselves from the ground and by some quirk of fate or luck there were no dead bodies within the dressing station. The doctor arranged for me to have some food and a drink of the awful 'coffee' and then I had to find my way back to the group that I now felt was my family.

I found them and duly reported to our leader who I had named General with the emphasis on the guttural 'G'. I thought he was going to give me a big slap on the back but he didn't, he just said 'Gut Tommy', and I joined the rest of the gang in the heart-rending job of opening up the cellars. We had to try and drag what was left of people into the open where they were examined for identifying marks and then piled up in huge squares. The final destination for these bodies would be one of the big water containers that had been built in various parts of the city. There they were burnt using gallons of petrol and oil. This was the only method of dealing with the huge numbers of bodies strewn across the rubble of what had been one of the most beautiful cities of Western Europe.

We were split into teams of four who would burrow into the mountains of bricks and mortar, find a cellar door and prise it with pickaxes and crowbars. Inside we found the victims, in most cases the bodies were shrivelled up to half their normal size or worse. Children under the age of three or four were impossible to identify at all, these tender human beings just melted in the heat of the oven they were sitting in. In the majority of cases the victims looked as though they had died peacefully through lack of oxygen, just losing consciousness and falling asleep in the process. After which the terrible heat took over and shrivelled them up. This was on the outskirts of the *Altstadt*, the old city, and it turned out to be the easy bit. Even the hardest of us was going to flinch as we got near to where the centre of the firestorm had been and where fierce fires were still raging.

The approach of darkness made the work impossible so the General called his gang to order and what remained of our forty-strong group trudged back to our position by the Railway embankment. This night we were treated much better. The General had been in contact with the main big boss of the area, who now came over to us to tell us that we would be sleeping in a couple of wagons for the duration of the exercise, and that even some blankets were to be supplied. Talk about organisation; we had food, drink and somewhere to kip. We still had no water for washing and if you had to answer the call of nature then it was just a question of making a hole in the rubble. We must have stunk like polecats, but so what, we were alive. So the second day ended.

The third day turned out to be a repeat of the day before. This was because we were still working in the same designated area, the main difference was there were more of us. Gangs had been bought in from far and wide, some on lorries and buses, others came along the only working railway line. Our sleeping wagons had been lifted off of the tracks, out of the way, by a giant crane. Everywhere I looked I could see men working in small gangs of up to a dozen men, usually escorted by a couple of armed guards.

I think the reason that our 'General' and those of us in his crew were left to our own devices was because we were doing the real dirty work of entering the shelters. As far as I could make out there were only about six or seven gangs employed on this task. Once a shelter was located we had the job of clearing the rubble from the doorway, this could take a couple of hours before we could uncover an entrance. Then came the horrendous task of forcing our way in, carefully managing the stairs that led to the basement below, and there we met the sight that so many of the men were unable to stand, the bodies of the unfortunates, sometimes seemingly untouched and in a kind of peaceful repose, but more often than not burnt to a crisp and smouldering shell. These experiences were to get much worse the nearer we got to the centre of the city.

Once we found the bodies, the General ordered the men who had not taken part in clearing access to the shelter to go down and try to bring the bodies that could be moved to the surface. Some of the corpses were so brittle that any attempt to move them resulted in a cloud of ash and dried flesh, and yet so methodical were these Germans that, where it was impossible to manhandle the bodies, they were ordered to stuff any part of the corpse that might help to identify the victim into a sack. It was all so gruesome that to describe what was going on with any degree of clarity is something that I, for one, can't do. I later heard that gangs of SS were used to gather these remains, I only heard about this through the chit chat in the evening so whether it's true or not I don't know. What I did know was that in spite of the fact that we were working day and night, our progress could only be measured in terms of yards per day. Even so, by the end of the third day we were so much nearer the fires that were still raging unabated, that nobody was looking forward to tomorrow's tasks.

There was a surprise in store for our gang when that evening we returned to the wagons: a shower wagon had arrived upon the scene and yet again I got special treatment. The General saw to it that I got first crack at washing and he also arranged for a medical orderly to bathe my bare skin where the blisters were breaking open. Why these blisters didn't fester up I don't know, perhaps it was the ointment that the German doctor had rubbed into my back. After we had our showers we had to put back on our filthy clothing, but it did feel good. I had a lot to thank our General for and I let him know that I was grateful even if we were unable to talk in anything but the most basic German words.

7

DAY FOUR

Up again with the first rays of light breaking through the dust and dirt. This morning instead of the usual men in charge of the field kitchen we were served by women which resulted in a lot of good natured cheering and calling out. Everyone formed up into a queue and the ladies doled out what appeared to be some form of stew, although I never came across anyone who had found even the smallest morsel of meat. To bulk it up there were these huge thick slices of black bread so much loved by the Krauts.

The second surprise was that we had a new leader this morning, in fact two of them, along with a young boy dressed up in an SS uniform and carrying a Schmeisser machine pistol. By the look of the lad he had never fired the thing, but experience told me that this might make him all the more dangerous if something untoward happened. This didn't seem to worry our two new masters who told the crew that we were to tackle a new sector of the city where it was thought there was a chance of finding survivors still alive. This news brought a kind of fresh life to the gang. We set off to a part of the city where there was a small square where what had been grass was now a bed of ash at least four inches thick. The houses surrounding this square were less damaged than those we had experienced up to now. As usual the roads were piled with masonry and other rubbish and we still had to find the shelter openings. So without any instructions from our new masters, the whole gang set to with a will that I am sure surprised the uniformed pair who were supposed to be instructing us. The General had trained us well to work together and it showed.

The first three shelters we uncovered were empty, but further examination of the third one revealed a tunnel leading to another shelter, but we couldn't get through because the roof had collapsed. We returned to the surface and one of our new leaders decided to have a look for himself. We could all tell that the man didn't want to venture underground, probably because of the damage it would do to his nicely creased jet-black uniform. But his mate, who was obviously his senior, ordered him down. The result was that we were to try to clear the tunnel. Then came the job of scouting around for timber to shore up the tunnel.

Later that afternoon three of our gang broke through and found these four women and two small girls huddled up together and still alive. Even the guards cheered themselves hoarse. It took an hour to get them to the surface but we all felt like heroes, there were no enemies, no hatred, just this sense of utter fulfillment that the rescue of these people had been down to us, that's how I felt and I am certain that every one of us had the same reaction. Sadly this was a one-off event. In spite of all the backbreaking toil this was the only time our group found people alive. We returned to the wagons that evening to be greeted by the General who had heard about the rescue.

After we had eaten the General came up to me with another short stocky German in an army uniform. This lad could speak really good English and, interpreting for the General, told me that tomorrow I was supposed to join a batch of British POWs, but if I wished I could stay with the group for another day. My first reaction was 'Good, can't wait to get back to my own mob'. Then I began to think about the 'what ifs'. What if they found out about me and Harry and that sentence that still had to be carried out. I told them I would like it better to stay with the group for another day. The General gave me a look but said nothing.

After much thought I decided that come feeding time tomorrow I would try to stuff as much of the black bread as I could in the pockets of the German greatcoat I was wearing and await the chance to lose myself. Beyond that I had no plan.

8

DAY FIVE

Day five and we were back under the command of our General. There was no sign of the other two men and the boy. Today there were special orders: we were to try to gain entry into one of the main communal shelters on the edge of the *Altstadt*. The General didn't think it was possible because of the heat which was still very intense. However he had his orders to see if some progress could be made, and see he would.

With the General leading the way, off we set in the direction of streets where sheets of flame were still shooting a hundred feet or so up into the sky. This time we were accompanied by a water truck with bags of wet rags and towels. The nearer we got, the hotter it got until the General called a halt and pointed to a still smouldering twenty foot high heap of rubble. The water-cart was still being manhandled over the piles of broken buildings, the path that had been cleared wasn't wide enough and indeed the cart never did reach our position. The general ordered half of us back into the cooler air whilst the remainder set about the task of trying to clear a way through to the entrance door. He kept us working like this in twenty minute shifts and in this manner progress was made until we all retired some hundred yards back for a midday break.

While we were sitting and lounging about, another gang of around fifty men turned up and after a short conflab the General got them into clearing the way to where it is thought the entrance to the shelter might be. The rest of us went on enjoying the break, but it came to an end when the General called over three of his German associates and signalled to me, 'Come Tommy', then made a sign for me to discard the shovel I was carrying and handed over a long crowbar, about five feet of inch-and-a-half-thick metal with a claw at one end. The other gang had uncovered the entrance and marched off, leaving us, who were now considered as specialists. The General says to me, 'In here very bad Tommy, very hot'.

The door was a massive affair, it had been bolted from the outside which was the general practice to prevent overcrowding. This was OK in theory but if there's nobody left on the outside to unbolt the door the people inside are in trouble.

It took the whole of the afternoon wielding sledgehammers trying to prise an opening. It was so hot that, this time, the General changed us around at fifteen minute intervals. So finally there were two of us on the end of the crowbar when with a creak it moved. The door opened the first inch or so, there was a large hissing sound and the surrounding dust was sucked into the opening. As the gap widened, so a terrible smell hit us. Everyone moved back and the General gave us time to recover our wits. Then he signalled to his four chosen men, which included me, and we continued the job of opening the heavy metal door. Slowly the horror inside became visible. There were no real complete bodies, only bones and scorched articles of clothing matted together on the floor and stuck together by a sort of jelly substance. There was no flesh visible, what had once been a congregation of people sheltering from the horror above them was now a glutinous mass of solidified fat and bones swimming around, inches thick, on the floor. The General signaled us to get out and got the rest of the gang to close the door as best they could.

Now we all understood what the cellars right in the centre of the city would reveal as their turn came to be opened. Although even on the fifth day we knew it was far too hot to venture into the area that we knew had been the central aiming point for the first two raids.

Gone were the high spirits that we had experienced the day before when we had released the women and girls from their living grave. Darkness began to fall and we marched back to the railway line. It was a very

subdued and sombre lot that queued up for the nightly
ration of soup, bread and the interminable coffee.

Before we turned in for the night the General came
over to me, 'Tommy, morgen sie gefangenenlager.'
He was telling me that in the morning I would go
back to the prison camp. I told him in my pidgeon
German that I understood. After a moment I held out
my hand to the man, it was not that I had fallen in
love with him but I respected him. We shook hands
and he said quite quietly 'Gut Tommy', and marched
off. That was the last I saw of him, I never discovered
his real name but I had the feeling that it amused him
when I addressed him as 'General'.

Now I had another problem to think about: how
to disengage myself from this party of men and make
my way over the bridge and try to walk eastwards. I
had given up the idea of walking to the west, it was
too far, whilst eastwards, during the silence of the
night, you could hear the rattle of machine guns quite
clearly, they couldn't have been more than twenty or
thirty miles away. So that was the way to go, I had no
alternative unless I took the chance that the Germans
would not discover that I had been condemned to
death for sabotage, and that was a chance I didn't feel
happy about taking.

9

DAY SIX

I was out of the Railway yard before light the next morning and making my way towards what I thought must be the north side of the City. I made my way unchallenged through the flow of people moving westwards, pushing small handcarts, prams, anything on wheels into which they had crammed their most treasured belongings. They were trying to put as much distance between themselves and the vengeful and menacing soldiers of the Red Army as possible. It was this trail that I followed except that instead of travelling westwards with them I was moving against the tide. I was still in luck when I got to the bridge. I had expected to find it guarded by the police or the army, but no, just this never ending trail of people.

As the morning got lighter so did the mass of refugees get thicker, it seemed to me that the whole of Germany was on the move. And so, slowly, I continued my way east until I reached an empty building and slipped in and found some paper and rags and laid down for the rest of the day, sleeping in

fits and starts and now and again taking a bite of the
few crusts of black bread that I had managed to save.

On the second day I must have covered a further
twenty miles or so, I was now off the main road, away
from the lines of refugees and later in the afternoon I
ate the last of the bread, and found shelter. That night
I could see the night sky still lit up by the burning
embers of what had once been Dresden. If I was
captured by any group of Germans I didn't fancy my
chances of survival when they discovered that I was
an 'Englander'. It was on the third day, the earth was
stone hard with frost and snow, I was trudging over
some fields, and then, almost as if it was on top of
me, I heard the unmistakable rattle of a machine gun.
There they were, about a hundred Russians climbing
through the bushes at the side of the field. I waved my
arms and realised as I started waving that this might
well be the moment of truth but I was so tired and
hungry that I don't think I cared.

They didn't shoot me. That night I was put in a
sort of cage with some Germans and a mixture
of displaced persons. Once again my luck held
as I demonstrated my usefulness by applying my
mechanical expertise to the problem of getting their
American Chevrolet lorries started and under way.
If they went wrong the Russians gave up trying to
fix them and resorted to pushing them or towing

them with horses. Fixing them was a simple matter of wiping dry the distributor leads and the internals and, hey presto, these utterly forgiving instruments of transport burst into life. After that I could do no wrong.

It must have been about two days after I made contact, I had my head in the bowels of a Chevy five-tonner trying to extract a set of plugs that had rusted in when one of the Russian officers approached me. He spoke to me in French, I recognised the lingo but nothing of what he was saying so I just said to him 'Anglais, non comprend France'. These four words were my limit, but his eyes lit up and he offered me his hand, which, I might add, was spotlessly clean whereas mine was covered in grease and oil, but he shook it all the same. 'Moment' he said, and disappeared to turn up half an hour later with another man who turned out to be German but was, like the Frenchie, dolled out in Russian kit. 'Englander?' says the Kraut by way of greeting. 'Ya, ich bin Englander.' Whereupon he gave forth in fairly good English. In answer to his questions I told him the tale about my misfortunes and how me and Harry had escaped by the skin of our teeth but that, alas, Harry wasn't as lucky as me.

After we had finished chatting he took me back to the command centre which, unlike it would have been in the British army, was only about two hundred yards to the rear. Two women and a man dressed my blisters, which were still open on my back. Then they gave me a clean shirt, taking the German overcoat and giving me one of the super warm quilted jackets. Then one of the women escorted me back to the lot who had picked me up and from there on I assumed that I was expected to go on making myself generally useful to the Russian war effort, and having nothing better to do I got stuck in with a will, why not? I was being fed and watered which, above all else, was what mattered.

Any opposition to the lot I was with was only spasmodic, a brief exchange of machine-gun fire and the small forces of Germans were speedily eliminated without too much ado. I stayed with this mob of Russians for the next eight to ten weeks until unification occurred along a stretch of river where an Allied force was already in situ.

At last, with much handshaking and well wishes, I was finally ferried across the river to be stuck on the back of a dispatch rider's motor cycle and whisked off to another enormous transit camp. Where I was I don't know and never cared, my war was over.

I am now back in the present, I am ninety-three years old and have lived with this part of my life for a month, trying to remember and write about it.

As I delve into my memory flashes come and go, I wake up in the middle of the night remembering sometimes disjointed phases of the experiences I went through. I remember the transit camp mainly because of one incident. The camp was brim full of displaced persons from every nation in Europe, stumbling about, looking at notice boards written in every language. There were huge marquees where people huddled together to keep warm and dry from the rain and sleet and there were the open-sided food tents, and it was in one of these that three big wooden casks of condensed milk were standing with their lids off, surrounded by people putting their hands into the gooey mass, then licking their fingers clean. My grubby hands went into the bin like the rest, everyone wanted to taste the sweet concoction. That night was spent huddled up on the grass floor of one of the marquees, freezing cold, but it represented food and shelter, and no bombs or machine-guns.

This all went on for two more days. Then I was suddenly plucked out of the crowds and given a brief interview by a British officer who put my back up so much that I stood up and walked out of the tent. Later, I was told by a sergeant that I was to stand by and be ready to board the next plane to Blighty.

There is so much that I have missed out in this narrative. Memories still flash back to me. In

Dresden, during the bombing, I remember arriving at what must have been a lovely open space, grassy and slightly wooded. I remember that the branches of the trees were starting to smoulder, people were milling around and that I left it because I thought it was getting too crowded for safety. I cannot remember which day this happened, I was on my own, so much happened and it was so long ago. There were other instances of which, while I can get a shadow of a memory, nothing concrete remains. Everything was overwhelmed by the gruesome tasks that we performed. It is the sheer horror that remains burned into my memory and, like the fires themselves, impossible to extinguish.

AFTERWORD

WAS THIS THE GREATEST WAR CRIME OF ALL?

The only reason for keeping this atrocity in the public eye is to horrify people so much that they never again allow their representatives to order such crimes. There is no excuse for the men who ordered this terrible event to be carried out. From the moment they bombed Hamburg they collected plenty of evidence as to what would happen to the civilians who were to bear the brunt of the raids. By the time of the bombing of Dresden the formula for the mass murder of civilians had been brought to a fine art. The commanders had developed a technique: first of all fires are started; then canyons of devastated buildings are created to draw the air to feed the inferno thus creating the winds and the fire storm; finally come the blockbusters that demolish everything and trap the helpless victims inside shelters that turn into ovens from which there is no escape. Ironically the ghastly events that I have tried to describe in these pages took place on the Christian holidays of Shrove Tuesday and Ash Wednesday.

I have every respect for the brave lads of the RAF who flew the bombers, they were under orders and, as a soldier, I know that orders are there to be obeyed. But, it is my belief that in the act of destroying the evil of the Third Reich we employed further and more terrible evils, although I know that not everybody agrees with me. As a nation I feel that the British people still have to face up to the satanic acts that were committed in their name. Above all else I wish to live to see a doctrine enforced by law that this nation will never again turn civilians into targets to create terror. I could say that I wish to live to see that war between nations stops for ever, but I am a realist and a firm believer that if an ogre like Hitler rears its head then that head should be cut off as speedily as possible. I am not a pacifist.

Rifleman V J Gregg 6913933. 2nd Battalion The Rifle Brigade & 10th Parachute Regiment, Army Air Corps. 1937–1946.

Victor Gregg
Swanmore, Hampshire
2013

A NOTE ON THE AUTHORS

Victor Gregg was born in in London in 1919 and joined the army in 1937, serving first with the Rifle Brigade in India and Palestine, before service in the Western Desert. Later, with the Parachute Regiment, he saw action in Italy and at the Battle of Arnhem, where he was taken prisoner and sentenced to death in Dresden, where, ironically, he was saved from execution by the Allied bombing of the city. He was demobilised in 1946.

Gregg wrote a trilogy of memoirs: *King's Cross Kid*; *Rifleman*; and *Soldier, Spy* about his life as a demobbed solider returning to civilian life and all the challenges that entailed. He wrote *Dresden, A Survivor's Story* to mark the anniversary of the bombing of Dresden which took place between 13 and 15 February 1945.

Rick Stroud is a writer and film director. As well as working with Victor Gregg on his memoirs, he is the author of *The Book of the Moon, The Phantom Army of Alamein, Kidnap in Crete* and *Lonely Courage*. He lives in London.

ALSO AVAILABLE
BY THE AUTHOR

RIFLEMAN
A front-line life from Alamein and
Dresden to the fall of the Berlin Wall

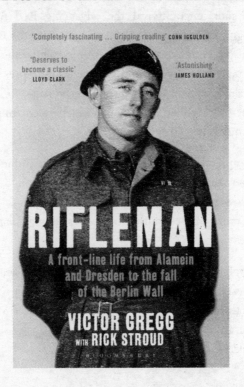

'Completely fascinating ... Gripping reading' CONN IGGULDEN

'Deserves to
become a classic'
LLOYD CLARK

'Astonishing'
JAMES HOLLAND

RIFLEMAN
A front-line life from Alamein
and Dresden to the fall
of the Berlin Wall

VICTOR GREGG
with RICK STROUD

BLOOMSBURY

On his eighteenth birthday in 1937, Victor Gregg enlisted in the Rifle Brigade and began a life of adventure. A soldier throughout the Second World War, he saw action across North Africa, was a driver for the Long Range Desert Group and fought at the Battle of Alamein. Taken into captivity at the Battle of Arnhem in 1944, he was sentenced to death for sabotaging a Dresden factory; he escaped only when the Allies' infamous air raid blew apart his prison and soon encountered the advancing Red Army. Gregg's fascinating tale does not end with the war – he also recounts his later adventures behind the Iron Curtain, offering behind-the-scenes glimpses into the shadowy world of Cold War espionage. *Rifleman* is the extraordinary story of an independent-minded and quick-witted survivor.

'Completely fascinating . . . It has an immediate power throughout that makes war fiction a pale shadow of the real thing'

Conn Iggulden, author of the bestselling *Conqueror* series

'A gripping life-story: an incident-packed account of heartache, violence and cunning by a man whose will to survive and unbreakable optimism are a true inspiration'

Independent

KING'S CROSS KID
A London Childhood Between the Wars

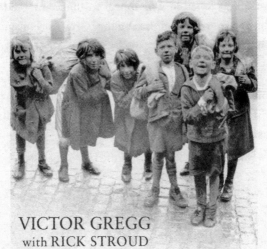

'One of the last voices of a vital generation' Conn Iggulden
'Intensely moving' ★★★★ *Mail on Sunday*

King's Cross Kid

A Childhood Between the Wars

VICTOR GREGG
with RICK STROUD

BLOOMSBURY

Born in 1919, Victor Gregg has had a rich and fascinating life. *King's Cross Kid* follows his London childhood from the age of five, when life was so hard that the Salvation Army arranged for young Vic to be taken to the Shaftesbury Home for Destitute Children. Home again a year later, the scallywag years of late childhood began. Then, after the years of street gangs and run-ins with the law, Vic leaves school at fourteen and his real adventures start, and with them a working-class apprenticeship in survival.

Ending with his enlistment in the army on the day of his eighteenth birthday, this prequel to the bestselling *Rifleman* will appeal to the many readers who were charmed by Victor Gregg's engaging, honest and warm voice.

'Evocative, detailed and unsentimental – gets us wonderfully close-up to the London of the 1930s viewed through the unblinking eyes of a working-class boy relishing every new experience'
   David Kynaston

SOLDIER, SPY
A Survivor's Tale

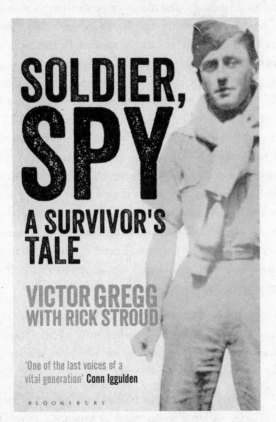

SOLDIER,
SPY

A SURVIVOR'S
TALE

VICTOR GREGG
WITH RICK STROUD

'One of the last voices of a
vital generation' **Conn Iggulden**

BLOOMSBURY

Beginning in 1946, when Victor Gregg was demobbed after the end of the Second World War and deposited in London Paddington, *Soldier, Spy* is the story of a soldier returning to civilian life and all the challenges it entails.

Facing a new and ever-changing London, a shifting political landscape and plenty of opportunities to make a few bob, repairing the bomb damage and doing construction work on the Festival of Britain site, Vic moves from one job and pastime to the next, becoming by turns cyclist, builder, decorator, trade union official, Communist Party member and long-distance lorry driver. Finally he is offered 'a nice clean job' as chauffeur to the chairman of the Moscow Narodny Bank in which he will be able to return home to his wife and children every night. However, there is more to his new employers than meets the eye, and it is not long before his wartime work with the Long Range Desert group catches up with him in the form of an approach from the security services. Lured by the excitement his postwar life has lacked, Vic adds spy to his roster of employments, risking everything in the process.

'Completely fascinating … It has an immediate power throughout that makes war fiction a pale shadow of the real thing' Conn Iggulden, author of the bestselling *Conqueror* series

'A gripping life-story: an incident-packed account of heartache, violence and cunning by a man whose will to survive and unbreakable optimism are a true inspiration'
   Independent

Victor Gregg takes us behind the scenes of this unforgiving terrain, to the sangars rather than the trenches, in an astonishing first-hand account of unfolding action. Through tender friendships and tea runs, devastating news from home and visible enemies on the horizon, Gregg goes beyond the graphic descriptions of injuries and front line action to show the psychological impact of daily life both on and off the battlefield.

Operation Compass was the first large Allied military operation of the Western Desert Campaign (1940–1943) during the Second World War.

The Western Desert Force, composed of around 30,000 men from British and other Commonwealth forces, advanced from Mersa Matruh on a five-day raid against the Italian positions of the 10th Army. Operation Compass continued long beyond its original limitations in order to exploit British success.

SECOND BATTLE OF
EL ALAMEIN
Snapshots of War Ebook Series

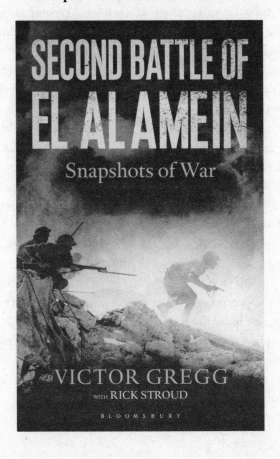

Victor Gregg, after an absence of eight months of service, is offered a promotion which he promptly turns down, saying, 'You will notice from a glance at my records that I have on at least three previous occasions turned down the offer of advancement. I just wish to fight out this war in the company of the lads who I call my mates, and they are all in the carriers.'

The Second Battle of El Alamein, Egypt (23 October–11 November 1942) was a decisive battle in the Second World War. With the Allies victorious, it marked the watershed of the Western Desert Campaign, causing Winston Churchill to proclaim 'Before Alamein we never had a victory. After Alamein we never had a defeat.'

The British victory turned the tide in the North African Campaign and ended the Axis threat to Egypt, the Suez Canal and the Middle Eastern and Persian oil fields via North Africa.

In this first-hand account, Gregg's words celebrate the unprecedented comraderies of war, but tight-knit groups make for very personal tragedies. He bravely unpicks not only the action of war, but the reaction of the normal men in extraordinary circumstances, trying to maintain sanity amongst the debris of corpses.

BATTLE OF ARNHEM
Snapshots of War Ebook Series

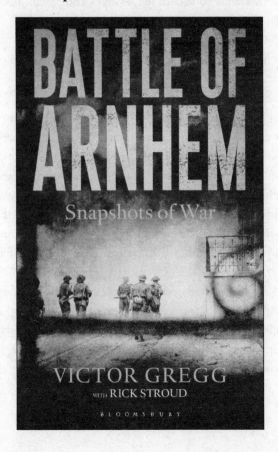

This is the story of how Victor Gregg switched from being a rifleman to a birdman.

After sweeping through France and Belgium in the summer of 1944, the Allies were poised to enter the Netherlands to secure key bridges and towns along the Allied axis of advance.

Gregg and his fellow riflemen are asked to volunteer for the Parachute Regiment, the staunch 'once a rifleman always a rifleman' overruled by a promise of extra leave.

The British airborne forces landed some distance from their objectives and were quickly hampered by unexpected resistance. Only a small force was able to reach the Arnhem road bridge, and reinforcements were unable to advance north as quickly as anticipated, therefore failing to relieve the airborne troops according to schedule. After nine days of fighting, the shattered remains of the British 1st Airborne Division were withdrawn.

The troops had been up against unimaginable odds, with countless tragic losses along the way. Gregg is subsequently captured and sent to a prisoner of war camp in Dresden, where the infamous and tragic bombings were about to begin.